- ABOUT MYSELF 6
- CHAPTER 1 EMOTIONAL INTELLIGENCE 8
  - INTRODUCTION 10
  - WHAT IS EMOTIONAL INTELLIGENCE? 12
  - TYPES OF COMMUNICATION 19
  - REAL-LIFE EXAMPLE 25
  - EQ ON TEAM MANAGEMENT 33
  - THE 4 EXTREMES 40
  - ACTION-REACTION 58
  - DEEP BREATHING EXERCISES 73
  - POCKET READER 78
  - ONLINE TESTS 82
  - EQ CONCLUSION 84
- CHAPTER 2 HOW TO PREPARE FOR YOUR JOB INTERVIEW 86
  - INTRODUCTION 88
  - PREPARE FOR YOUR INTERVIEW 90
  - THE FIRST INTERVIEW 97
  - DRESS CODE AND POSTURE 100
  - INTERVIEWER BODY LANGUAGE 109
  - QUESTION THE INTERVIEWER 115
  - SALARY AND BENEFITS 119
- CHAPTER 3 HOW TO DO A PROPER JOB INTERVIEW 126
  - INTRODUCTION 128
  - PREPARE FOR YOUR INTERVIEW 130
  - JOB ADVERTISEMENT 132
  - CV PYRAMID 137
  - PREPARE THE INTERVIEW 142
  - THE INTERVIEW 158
- WRAPPING UP 162

FREE DOWNLOAD

Contrary to popular belief, your resume and presentation letter will not get you that desired job opportunity. Use this free document to help you prepare for the interview and keep them organized at the same time.

Sign up for the author´s New Releases mailing list and get a free copy of the "Get a Job organizer"

Click here to get started https://www.uyourp.com/job-interview-organizer/

Unlock your potential in the workplace – Emotional intelligence & job interviews - Volume 1 by Daniel Dias

Published by Amazon

www.uyourp.com

© 2019 Daniel Dias

All rights reserved. No portion of this book may be reproduced in any form without permission from the publisher, except as permitted by U.S. copyright law. For permissions contact:

uyourp@gmail.com

You are allowed to print page 79 and pages 145 to 156.

Ebook ASIN: B07VCB6CV6

ABOUT MYSELF

I am an Engineer Manager with more than 15 years' experience in the Automotive and Aerospace industries. Worked and lived in multiple countries. I also possess several management degrees that allow me to be a better leader, better professional, and person.

My passion is to lead multicultural teams to achieve success. I can tell you there is usually a better, smarter way to do things, to be assertive and go beyond your expectations if you believe in yourself, trust your instincts, let go of the fear of failure, be open to learning new things, and don't let others push you back.

I will share the knowledge and tools I used by working in several countries and corporations as an engineer and manager. I intend to be as forthcoming as possible, crude, to say things as they really are and how they worked for me. I gathered valuable information from my experience and from research to lay it here down for you in a simple, down to earth manner. You will be able to apply it starting day one. I worked with all kinds of people in different positions in a company, from the shop floor to

CEOs/Company owners, with different cultures, from different countries and different generations. I failed as much as I succeeded.

I made mistakes, made breakthroughs, embraced both, and learned with both. I am here to help you. My goal is to empower you to have a new perspective, become smarter, see the signs in front of you, and grab the opportunities. I had some help during my work life, and now that I am in my 40s, I decided it is time to share my knowledge with others.

Continuing to evolve in my career, always learning and open to new experiences and challenges. Workplaces are complex and in movement, not static places where one rule applies to all. Come and learn how to navigate through rough water to get to your desired goal.

Chapter 1
EMOTIONAL INTELLIGENCE

INTRODUCTION

What is Emotional Intelligence (EQ)? How is it important and how it has an influence on you and your career?

I will explain in detail what EQ is, the importance it has on your career, show you several examples of different kinds of situations, the way I think you should handle them and the expected result. This is based on my professional experience, professionals I talked to and studies I read about.

To master EQ is extremely important and it will make the difference between you staying in your position, lose it or moving up quickly on your career. Professionals, who master Emotional Intelligence, have strong social awareness, thrive and have respect from their peers. When you don't have a sharp EQ is like you are driving in a heavy fog road that you only notice danger or a warning when you are about to hit something and by that time is too late to avoid it. When you have EQ and use it is like flying high and be able to see all the obstacles and see what is around you from miles away.

WHAT IS EMOTIONAL INTELLIGENCE?

Figure 1 - Photo courtesy of pixabay

You probably hear about Emotional intelligence (EQ) before but you probably don't know what it is or when and how to use it properly.

As individuals, our success and the success in the role we play today depends on our ability to read other people's signals and react appropriately to them. There are a lot of areas in life that a sharp EQ is important, like in your personal relationships, when playing sports, but I am going to talk about those areas where I have experience at, as a professional and as an Engineer Manager, leading a team to success.

Before I share my personal experience let me show you how the concept of Emotional Intelligence (EQ) appeared in our society? Basically, this was the order of events:

1920's	IQ started
1985	Dr. Reuven Bar-on, clinical psychologist and W.L. Payne started to include the IQ concept in his work.
1990	John Mayer and Peter Salovey both psychologists identified EQ as not being the same as having intellectual ability
1995	EQ becomes a worldwide concept mostly because of books published by Daniel Goleman.

Our level of intelligence is usually measured nowadays by our IQ. There are many tests and sites online mentioning you can improve your IQ, but what I read about, is that out IQ is set by the age of 3, after that it does not change much. So how can you improve your work performance if you can barely change your IQ anymore? The answer is to improve your EQ.

How do you explain people with high IQ not moving up on their career, not being great leaders and people not following them? Because they can act very emotionally at times, say the wrong thing at the wrong time and not listen. They lack emotional intelligence. Having High IQ doesn't mean you have High EQ. We all know very smart professionals, brains in their area but who are rude, unsocial, not a people person. We don't all grow up to be great speakers or sellers or good at negotiations, but having a good control of your emotions will contribute to all areas of your life. So how do we do that? I will show you as we move forward in the book.

First, let me show you an example I have on a company I worked for.

I had colleagues that were somehow smart but arrogant, didn't really know about the technical things we were doing or developing and had the most stupid ideas for a new process or new ways to do things. You could see right away they wouldn't work but these colleagues of mine could sell the idea very well and if you would listen to them, even you could get hypnotized with what they say because they know how to please and work people. They could even convince you. They had a good EQ and I call them good car salesmen.

> IQ is set by the age of 3, after that it does not change much.

I also had very smart colleagues who really knew what they were talking about and they knew about the subject. The problem was their ability to keep it together when things didn't go the way they planned. They lashed out to their workers because they have a bad day or are being pressured by upper management.

You can have good EQ, control your emotions and have social awareness, anyone can. I remember the time I could not see things through the fog, I could feel inside something was wrong, but not really put my finger on it.

WHAT IS THE EQ DEFINITION?

Figure 2 - Photo courtesy of rawpixel

Daniel Goleman (mainly responsible for EQ to become a Worldwide phenomenon due to his book) from the Institute for Health and Human Potential defined EQ as:

"EQ is the ability to recognize, understand and manage our own emotions; Recognize, understand and influence the emotions of others."

EQ can be radically changed, learned and used as a very strong asset to move on your career, in relationships and even in sports and area in life.

I am sure you know people who you think don't have an IQ as higher as you, who cannot do what you do or see what you see but who can have high EQ and move faster on their career. They have the ability to keep calm and focus when things are hard or under fire, to be quiet when needed and to say the right thing at the right time in the right way. They can read people's emotions very well, listen, look you in the eyes and see what you are really saying. They have empathy, know when you are lying, keep good relations, avoid burning bridges with other people, customers, avoid conflicts in general and read a room very fast.

How do you think they do it? Don't you think experience people with good EQ feel fear, stress, sadness, rage, and other kind of emotions? Yes, they all do but they learn through training or/and experience how to react to those feelings and control them.

TYPES OF COMMUNICATION

Figure 3 - Photo courtesy of rawpixel

Let's talk first about the known types of communication. They are interconnected with our EQ and they can be used to better communicate with others as well as to better receive the communication from others.

The most respectful study on the importance of verbal and nonverbal messages was done by Prof. Albert Mehrabian of the University of California in Los Angeles in the 1970's and is still applied today. He said we usually have our feelings, attitudes, and beliefs about what someone says in a certain way, not by what they actually say, the actual words, but by their body language and tone of voice.

Prof. Albert Mehrabian then came up with the **7-38-55 rule** where 7% of what we say is spoken words, 38% is voice and tone and 55% is body language. This is why important conversations and negotiations should be done in person and not by phone or chat. He believed that if words and body language disagree, we should believe the body language.

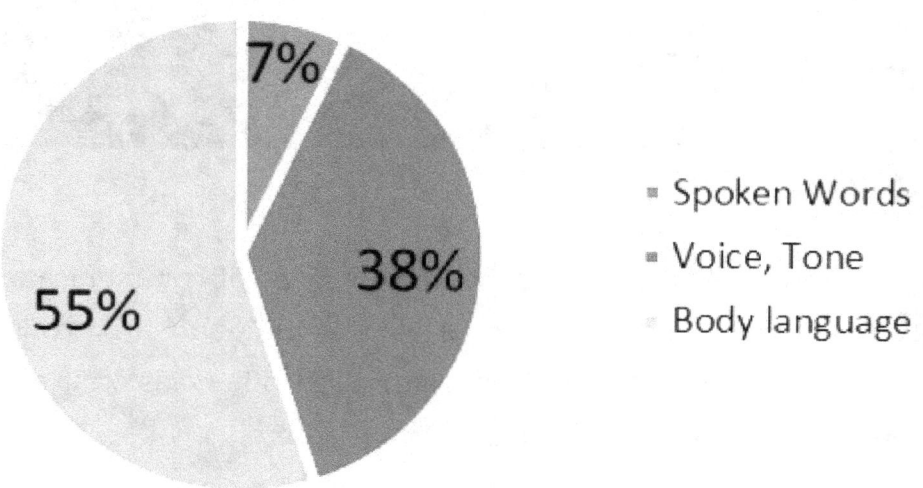

I remember many times giving a task to a person and in the end asking if they understood the task and the answer was yes, but the body language was clearly saying no. You could see it in the person's face and eyes. I even had one team member who usually shook his head sideways showing a clear no, while saying yes. So yes, do believe mainly in the body language.

Who didn't have any misunderstandings while on a chat, or email? As per this study, I can understand why. We lose 93% of our communication using only spoken words. Unfortunately, many people feel more comfortable behind a computer and prefer to send an email rather than picking the phone or having a talk face to face. I have seen it happen many times where are people seated side by side and are emailing each other. If possible always use the face to face method, unless you want to hide something and you know it will show in a face to face conversation.

Maybe you are thinking about using Video conferences instead of face to face meetings. Is it the same to have a video conference or being actually present? In my opinion, there is a big difference. It feels artificial, is

> "EQ is the ability to recognize, understand and manage our own emotions; Recognize, understand and influence the emotions of others."
> By Daniel Goleman

like eating something with peach flavor and actually eating a peach. You also cannot see everything, only what is framed on the screen, many times only the face and upper shoulder part, losing a lot of body language.

To have an idea of how much body language is important in a negotiation, there are experts whose only task is to be on very important negotiations observing the room and all people involved and taking notes to brief the CEO/manager at the end of the negotiation. Interesting don't you think? For someone to be on a meeting, just to measure you up, what you are really implying, feeling and hiding.

So why do we need EQ? We need it because we are reactive creatures. We react first and think later if we don't control our emotions.

So why do we react first and think later, it has to do how our brain is designed.
Our called emotional brain is located in the Limbic System and it is there since our ancestors, it is much older in our evolution. The Neocortex is more recent and it is where all cognitive abilities reside our IQ.

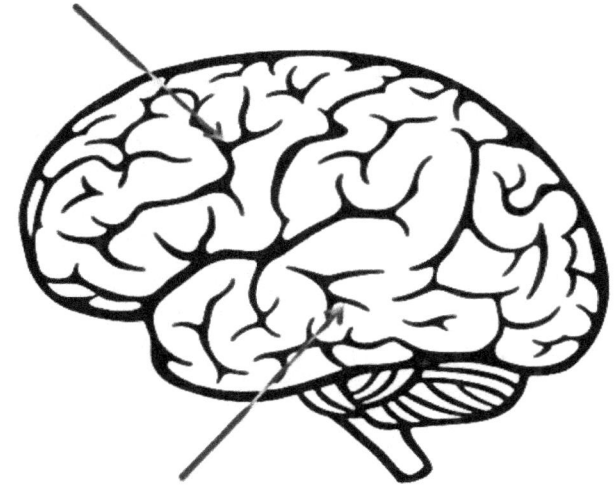

So we feel before we think which for our ancestors and nowadays, in dangerous situations is great. If our ancestors had a predator coming their way the emotional brain would turn on and send them running away to try to escape. They wouldn't stop and think first if they should go left or right or stay. If we let our emotions take over completely, the emotional brain will make us react in 3 ways, fight, flight or freeze. Our emotional reaction is also very connected to our emotional background how we were raised, our experiences, and the way we were brought up basically. It is very important also that you sleep well. Lack of sleep will make it more difficult to control your emotions.

We can control our emotions. It takes training, control, discipline and proper rest. Let me show you a real example on the next page.

REAL-LIFE EXAMPLE

Figure 4 - Photo courtesy of rawpixel

I had to change and adapt. When I started my first real job I can say I had low EQ, this was back in 2003. I still remember how I would be uncomfortable talking in front of a group of people. Doing a presentation for example it was an anxiety trigger.

I still remember when my boss back then told me that I had to train 20 people because he was not able to. I knew about the subject, I was an expert on it, but had never given training before.

I was introverted back then and so my anxiety level went high at that moment. I remember the time I felt uncomfortable just talking to my manager to grab an opportunity on the company, or saying that I am not available to work on the weekend even if I had very good reasons. I was young and naive and learned the hard way.

I learned a lot during the next following year, how to control more efficiently my emotions, have more social awareness and be smarter in the way I would use my new skills to favor me.

> We feel before we thing because or emotions are located in an older part of the brain called Limbic system.

I remember one episode I was asked to work on a weekend by Andrew, a senior manager because we were late on schedule and he wanted to show to his boss that he had a plan to improve the dates. He did not have any plan, any real one at least, but just by asking people to work on the weekend was like a smokescreen to show he was on top of it and if something went wrong he had time to come up with an excuse.

First, he asked me this on a Friday and secondly I had already told him I had plans but that I would gladly cancel them if it was really necessary like a plane is on the ground or one of our customers' needs this ASAP. I asked him what was needed, the plan, the expected result for the weekend and he had no clear answer, no plan, just wanted for me to show up and be on-site if necessary.

I suggested to him taking my laptop home and also that he could call me on my cell phone anytime if needed. He rejected that idea completely. He wanted me to present on-site no matter what. I said to him politely that I wouldn't come to work that weekend since my presence would not make any difference. The company would be paying for me to be there for nothing and I had to cancel my plans for the weekend. He did not like my response and left really upset. He did not like me very much after that. I was polite, calm, explain my point of view and listen to his.

You are only responsible for your own actions and emotions. Whatever others do or feel is not your concern as long you are assertive.

Later on that day, I was talking to my manager in his office and the General Manager was also inside talking with the company VP. Andrew, the senior manager that spoke with me before, entered the room and asked me again if I could come on the weekend in front of my manager, the GM, and the VP. His intention was to make me give under pressure and accept to go on the weekend. I was nervous, but I was able to remain calm and answered no again. The GM asked me why and I told him what I told Andrew. He agreed with me. Later that day he called me to his office and put me in charge of a new project. So be honest, truthful, assertive and professional. You never know who is listening. It could easily come the other way and the GM could have not agreed with me. I wouldn't change the way I am or work. I would start looking for another job at a different company that has values similar to mine.

I was able to control my emotions. It isn't always possible. I learned a lot in 15 years about controlling myself, my thought and my emotions.

You can also help your team members to be more assertive and strong. I had a team member who would always say yes when asked to work on the weekends by other managers. There is nothing wrong to show upper management that you will do overtime to help the business, but you do also have your personal life to think about. It was the 4th weekend in a row he was supporting the business. I knew he had a wife and family, so I called him aside and told him that if he couldn't come on the weekend, it was ok for him to say no. He had supported the company several times before. I told him if he had any problems, to come and talk with me.

I could see he needed time off and how the constant working was affecting his moral. He said no several times and I had to speak with the managers that were overloading him with work to stop doing that. He was happier, confident and the quality of his work improved. There are small things you can do to empower your team and this is one of them.

How did I control my emotions in that office when asked to work on the weekend? How can you show you are always in control and remain calm? How can you do that especially when you are being thrown under the bus when someone is trying to blame you for something that went wrong or ask you to do something you said you would not in front of a room full of people? It is not always easy. It takes time and experience, but it is not an impossible task. To achieve that you will need first to:

- Know how much you are worth to the company;
- Be ready to talk about your work anytime;
- If you don't know the answer to a certain question, say that you will investigate and come back in a certain time frame. If you are not sure, be sure;
- Be ready to admit a mistake was made. Have a solution for it and a way to avoid the same problem in the future;
- Be able to control your breathing and racing thoughts;
- Know what you can expect from people;
- Be assertive, not passive or aggressive;
- Read people intentions and the underline meaning of what they are saying;
- Learn to listen. It is ok to be in a meeting just hearing what is being said.
- Learn to observe what is around you and in front of you;

- Ask questions for clarification when needed and as many times necessary until everything is 100% clear;

I cannot offer you experience, only time can do that. I will guide you and show you what to do in a certain situation. What are usually other people's reactions? I will give you the tools and then the experience will make things come out more naturally.

For me, the experience gave me the tranquility I needed to deal with situations in which I would usually feel stressed.

Remember one thing when you are under pressure, no one has the power to make you feel uncomfortable, unwelcome or unease. You make that to yourself because you are not in control of your emotions. It takes time to have more Emotional Intelligence (EQ). You will have days where things don't go the way you planned. You will try things that do not work but you will start to see changes for the best from day one after you have read this book.

I have been talking about how EQ is important for you as a professional but EQ is also very important when managing a team. Your team is counting on you to be calm, direct, precise, fair and trustworthy. Keep this in mind,

- the first reason people leave the company is because of their direct manager. They leave the manager, not the company.

EQ ON TEAM MANAGEMENT

Figure 5 - Photo courtesy of rawpixel

I manage a group of very smart engineers from different countries, backgrounds, and even different generations. I have 20 years of old Engineers as well as +50-year-old engineers in my Team.

I believe that for anyone to be a good team leader or manager you need to:

- **HAVE EMPATHY AND RESPECT** –know your team members, know what makes them tick. Talking with them about other things than work makes a connection. Treat your team members with the respect and dignity they deserve.

- **COMMUNICATE** – have time to listen to your team members. Have regular one on one meetings. When they come to your office stop whatever you are doing and listen, don't continue working on your computer because that shows a lack of interest. That way you fail to read the body language and how your worker really feels. Be sure to follow-through if they bring up an issue that they are not happy with or concerned about.

- **BE FIRM AND FLEXIBLE** – you need to follow company policy, but inside the policy, you need to be flexible for your best team members. For my best team members, for example, I usually give them compensation time because they did a great job on a certain project or helped us improve schedule for example. On the other hand, I will not give compensation time to employees that just did their regular work, or even work extra hours to meet schedule because they slacked before.

- **SUPPORT** – Your team expects from your support, leadership, and guidance. You need to be able to find the answers to their questions and not just give an "I don't know" or "I will have a look at that later" answer and never giving them more feedback on the subject. Empower your team with the info and tools they need to succeed because if they succeed you succeed.

- **KEEP CALM WHEN UNDER PRESSURE** – I have seen it happen many times when a manager or team lead is under pressure by upper management and ends up lashing on the team. They do not filter the information, the bad energy and go on a rampage, demanding and talking rudely with their employees. This will alienate them. They will do less for you or just not care about doing a good job. Their trust in you will be shattered and to get that trust back will be extremely difficult. Remain calm if your team is late, reunite with them and have a plan to catch up. Find out why things are late and what can be done for that not to happen again. Praise their achievements and give spot rewards to your best team members.

- **APPRECIATE AND RECOGNIZE** – We know now that the first reason people leave their job is because of their direct manager. But why? Usually, they are not appreciated, not recognized, not promoted and don't feel like an important part of the company. They do not receive positive feedback, are feed up with all the broken promises and their suggestions constantly ignored. Be sure to recognize the talent on your team and do that recognition shortly after the event took place. Don't wait until the end of the year to do that if the event was 6 months before.

- **TALK IN PRIVATE WHEN YOU CRITICIZE AND EVEN PRAISE** –I see this many times. Managers criticizing team members in the presence of other co-workers. If you have to criticize an employee, do it at close doors, in private. If you are praising a team member, you can do it privately or in the presence of others, it depends. Make sure you know your employees. Most of the time I praise in the presence of their colleagues, to show my appreciation and to influence others to follow the example but I had a very shy employee before and they hate to be praised in the presence of others.

- **INVESTIGATE** – For example, if all of a sudden someone is constantly getting in late, investigate to find out why. Maybe he or she has a family issue. Don't rush to conclusions. Another example is if someone always makes the excuse that they are missing schedule because of IT issues, investigate, so you have all the facts and act accordingly.

- **KNOW WHAT THEY WANT** – Ask what they want and try to pave the road for them to get there.

- **TRUST AND GIVE AUTONOMY** – Show that you trust your team members and give them autonomy to reach a goal in their own way. Often managers that do not trust their team members will micromanage them. They always question their decisions and demand they ask for approval in everything they do. If you do this your team members will feel a lot of stress, anxiety and unable to do their work properly. They will eventually leave the company.

Can I always remain calm and in control when managing a team? Yes, on the outside, on the inside it is not always possible.

I remember when I told one of my team members about the constant bad quality of his work and the extremely long time he would take to make anything. I told him that several times and he never changed so I had to start a PIP (Performance Improvement Plan). My intention was to help him improve and give him a chance to step up.

I would sit down every week and give him weekly goals to check on his progress. His performance did not improve. One day he bursts into my office, talking in a very rude way, about an email I had sent him informing him he had missed a goal. He continued his behavior, asking why he got that email since in his opinion was improving. He was raising his voice and I told him in a calm, firm voice that he was not improving and showed him why. I informed him that I discussed that with him several times before and he called me a liar.

As you can imagine, on the inside I was fuming. I just wanted to kick him out of the room and the company building. My wish was to start raising my voice. Instead of doing that, I told him in a firm voice that he couldn't call me a liar, that he should go back to his desk and check the goals he had missed and come back when he was calmer.

He returned 15 min after, apologized and said he had family problems and was a little on the edge. I accepted his apologies and did not take it personal.

> You are responsible for your actions and emotions not for others, so just focus on being assertive and your own actions.

His performance improved somehow for some time but I had to let him go, unfortunately, because his behavior deteriorated again and he returned to his old habits.

Don't take things personally when you are running a business or a team. Keep calm and assertive all the time. You will gain their respect, loyalty and they will know they always have an open door to discuss anything without fearing consequences.

THE 4 EXTREMES

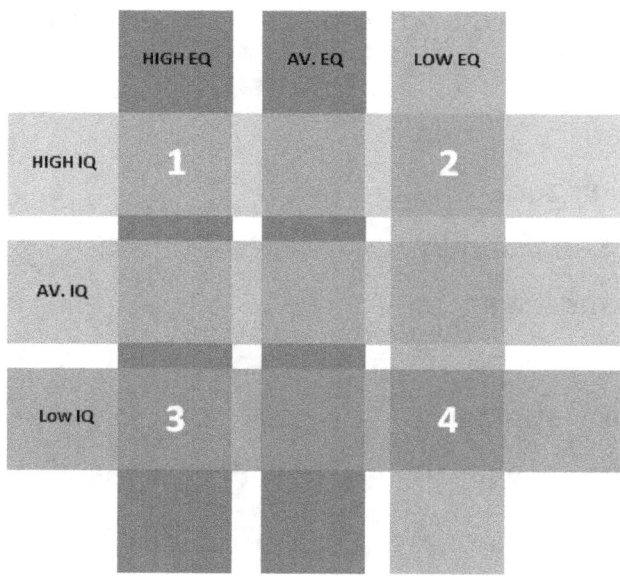

I found out after many years of experience and research that people can be easily categorized into 9 groups when it comes to EQ and IQ.

I will only talk about the 4 extremes of that group. Most people have average EQ and IQ. If you look at the extremes and learn to identify their behavior, you will grow your social awareness faster and identify the same patterns on the average groups.

GROUP 1 - HIGH IQ AND HIGH EQ

Figure 6 - Photo courtesy of pixabay

This is the best team member or manager you can have or be. Smart, listens to everyone's ideas, criticizes with facts, in a constructive manner and always remain calm when criticized or under pressure.

People who fit this group don't talk very much or just for the sake of talking, they are not much of a chit chat's person. They have a purpose and have an objective in mind for any conversation. Managers in this group have the ability to be like a water dam, to block stress when they are under pressure and to keep their team calm, sharp and focused on the job they have at hand. They don't lie to their team. They are open about the business situation and the company. They have a good way to let you know about the bad news and still are able to make you feel confident about the future. They have the right posture. They are calm and polite. They keep eye contact when talking to you and they use a low tone of voice. They transpire self-confidence.

They make you feel important and an essential member of the team. They help you move up on your career and will make you feel bad if you have a silly question or complaint about their management style. Also, they don't talk trash about other people or teams.

Let me tell you a story that happened to me. While working in another country, on that job I was in charge of a team of 20 engineers and there was another team, in another country, in charge of defining the processes and rules for us to follow.

There were times where the processes for us to follow did not really improve anything. Sometimes those processes would make our life more difficult but instead of talking badly about the team who made up the processes, I would try to explain to the team the point of view of the other team that laid down the new processes. I would let my team know that that was the process for us to follow at that moment and that we had to follow it the best we could. I remembered them we were working together for the same goal and that their concerns would be passed to the upper manager and we would try to emend the new processes.

I have watched many times managers always complaining and making bad remarks about other teams. That will lower morale and put people in a fighting mode instead of a cooperating mode.

If you fit in this category, that's spectacular, you are on your way to greatness and there is not much I can do to help you get better, experience will do that for you.

GROUP 2 - HIGH IQ AND LOW EQ

This group is divided into 2 types of personalities:

THE AGGRESSIVE:

Figure 7 - Photo courtesy of Moose

These people are very smart and know what they are talking about. They invent, they have ideas, they come with solutions you never thought before but there is a catch. They can be very rude, in your face, very defensive if you criticize one of their ideas and they try to keep all the information to themselves. They usually don't share their knowledge because they are insecure.

They are the only ones who know about a certain subject, the experts and think this will give them job security.

They tend to be narcissistic. They need admiration from others, only care about them, cannot handle criticism and have a sense of entitlement.

If you think about a manager, they usually lose their temper with the team easily, do not accept that they are wrong and do not stop defending their position.

Just a tip, <u>everyone is replaceable</u>, everyone can cost a lot of money to lose a key person but the company will go back on track in no time.

You can as a manager try to have this type of person change but is not usually easy or possible. They tend to leave the company when you warn them more than once about their behavior or end up with a disciplinary process.

> **People usually leave the company because of their direct manager**

On the other hand, If you have a manager like this, start thinking about changing jobs or departments, you will be exhausted and with no prospects of moving up in your career. Until you change the job or department have a look at your company policies to see if there is something you can do with the help of HR to stop this harassment. There is always someone above your manager, don't be afraid to make a complaint if something serious happens.

I remember when I was a just a design engineer and there was a manager that was assigned for a critical project. When the project started sinking, he insulted and screamed at people, right in their faces. They made a complaint to HR and eventually, the manager was called for his behavior and things were settled. So, know your company, internal policies and see where you can be helped if the behavior is serious from your manager.

If you fit this group you need to tackle your aggressive side, usually is connected to some kind of anxiety or frustration.

There are some books that can probably help you tackle aggressive behavior:

"<u>Beyond Anger: A Guide for Men: How to Free Yourself from the Grip of Anger and Get More Out of Life</u>";

"<u>The Anger Workbook for Women: How to Keep Your Anger from Undermining Your Self-Esteem, Your Emotional Balance, and Your Relationships</u>".

You can easily find them online for sale.

THE PASSIVES:

Figure 8 - Photo courtesy of Pragyan Bezbaruah

On the other hand people in this group can be very shy, not demanding their rights, being pushed by others, saying nothing is ever wrong, and "dying" whenever they have to talk to a crowd on a simple meeting. They are not able to read others properly and therefore they believe everyone is good and has good intentions.

I know managers who love this kind of professionals because they have low self-esteem thus allowing them to fly on the wings of these people's ideas. They get away with it by giving them a tap on their back and by making false promises that they never intended to keep. When questioned about those promises they blame others. HR is their favorite scapegoat.

When I have these employees on my team, I try to help them in a strategic way to make them more confident. I start by giving them small tasks that they can do by themselves and place them in small work teams. Later on, I take them to an important meeting so they can start to feel comfortable around people.

Treat them with respect, tact and give them a chance to change. I transformed one of my employees in such a way that she would take my place in important meetings when I wasn't available and make a presentation in public halls. When I met her, if I'd ask her to do one of those things, she would probably be petrified and resign on the same day.

Let's now imagine you have a shy manager. They are not able to confront anyone including their own team members. The team usually can manipulate managers on this group so they can do whatever they want to. They agree with anyone, even if they know they are wrong. They just need to be pushed a little further for them to crack and eventually give away.

If you have a boss like this and you like to manipulate him or her to your advantage, it can sound great now but in the end, it is not that great. The problem is, they don't have your back and they will not help you move up on your career. They are not going to help you find a solution to a current problem because they have to confront people in order to do that. Normally these kinds of leaders try to stay in the shadow, not to be noticed and will probably assign a team member to represent them in difficult situations.

On the other hand, if you fit in this group you really need to raise your self-confidence and realize how valuable you are. I am not able to help with that but, what I can say is, it does not matter what other people think about you. Believe in yourself and be strong, always keep moving forward. When you have a situation that makes you anxious, the only way to stop those anxious feelings is to expose yourself to those situations as much as possible. You will eventually become immune and feel comfortable.
You can also practice certain scenarios, do it in front of a mirror and ask a friend or family member to make a role play with you for example.

GROUP 3 - LOW IQ AND HIGH EQ

This group is divided into 2 types of personalities also:

THE DELUSIONAL:

Figure 9 - Photo courtesy of Craig Adderley

There are delusional employees and managers in every company. They think they are the best in what they do. No one understands them because they are dumb. They don't like to be criticized. Even though their ideas usually are not that good, they will sell them to anyone who is willing to listen.

If management is not careful and has no countermeasures in place for this kind of people, they can and will damage financially a company and their reputation. I have seen it happen many times. They will fail but before they do, they will convince everyone, including costumers their idea is bulletproof.

There will be eventually a time when everything falls like a deck of cards and they will blame everyone else including their allies. It's never their fault. Everyone else's is to blame. They will never admit they are wrong. Their idea was just implemented incorrectly.

They are usually called "brown noses". They are the ones who keep their jobs or even move up on their career not by their achievements but because of the ability to manipulate others and to make alliances to empower them and their ideas. They will claim your ideas as their own ideas and take credit for them. They will never praise an employee and usually, they will give bad annual reviews. I would say they are like cancer in a company.

They are like ghosts, unreachable. No one knows where they are when they are to blame when their input is needed to figure out an urgent solution or a clarification is required. You will also notice they are always extremely busy. They try to be involved in as many things as possible in the company, so they can give the illusion they are indispensables.

If you fit in this category you are going for a surprise. Hold on tight because you are going to fall big and it will be worse if you are on a high hierarchy in the company. You need to try to be more humble, modest and realize you work in a team and only as a team you can really succeed and be admired.

I have seen people rising faster than me, not because of their job qualities, but because they will step on everyone to get where they want and bootlick all the way. I knew exactly what I needed to do to move faster also, I had the opportunity, the chance, but I choose the correct path, the hardest road. I can walk head high, look into my son and wife's eyes and be proud of everything I accomplished because it was due to my hard work. If I don't know something, I will study it and not rest until I know everything that there is to know about it. I took the blame when it was for me to be blamed and I helped others to succeed along the way. You just have to choose what kind of person you are.

THE "DOWN TO EARTH":

Figure 10 - Photo courtesy of rawpixel

Some company owners and managers know their limitations, they know they are not that smart but are smart enough to hire the smartest and loyal people there is and give them the freedom, paycheck, benefits and the power to do their jobs.

Usually, you will find 2 scenarios when you have a manager who fits this group. In the first scenario, they promote you, ensure you move on your career and support you. In the second scenario, they stall you and try to keep you underneath them as much as possible because it suits them and their own selfish objectives. They fly on your wing.

They are very friendly, polite and talk with you a lot in private to make you feel sure they have your back. They tell you "secrets" and "rumors", anything to make them gain your trust and make you feel special. They also give the illusion they are very busy all the time.

If you are a manager who fits in this group try to get some education and training. Support your team as much as possible. You can easily be seen as a great leader and admired. If you are just an employee, keep in your "lane". Do what you feel comfortable doing and what you are good at.

GROUP 4 - LOW IQ AND LOW EQ

Figure 11 - Photo courtesy of Mentatdgt

What a disaster. Blame HR and who hired this employee, they were probably using a blindfold when they hired him or her. They will do anything to keep their job and to take the focus out of them.

I used to have one person like this on my team that I inherited when I was promoted. They will lie, blame others, blame the computer, anything goes. My advice for you is unless there is a place in the company where they can be transferred and do a good job if you have one employee that fits this group, raise a PIP (Performance Improvement Plan) and thinks about layoff this person. Sometimes they are just in the wrong department. You will be doing them a favor, because one thing I notice is, these employees suffer from lots of stress while trying to keep in the shadow.

If you fit this category, believe me, it is not worth the stress of trying to hide to stay in your current job. Try to do something you love to do, you will be happier.

ACTION-REACTION

Figure 12 - Photo courtesy of pixabay

Newston's third law talks about the concept of Action-Reaction. Basically, he said that for every action there is a reaction. If you think about the day to day things you see that is true. For example, if you kick a soccer ball the ball will move, if you let an egg fall it will crack or if you are rude to someone, that person will probably be rude to you. The reaction can be several to some action, depending on numerous factors.

Is there a proper reaction to an action, to an event? Yes and no. There is definitely an innumerous number of ways you can react to an event, and maybe they are all correct. I am not going to give you the only reaction possible but instead, show you some examples for you to have an idea of what to do or say.

Like I said, they are just real-life examples that you can use and adjust to your particular situation and personality. They will empower you, give you control and make you look good in the end.

So let me show you 4 common situations and how I think you should react. I used these more than once and it really worked.

SCREAM AT YOU

Figure 13 - Photo courtesy of Craig Adderley

So imagine the following situation: You are in a meeting, with your boss or a colleague and they are screaming at you or you work at customer service, for example, and you have an unhappy customer on the phone. The way to react is basically the same whenever someone is screaming at you.

When someone screams at you, the first instinctive thing to do is to scream back, especially if you are being blamed for something and it is not your fault. Breathe in and out a couple of times and count to 5 to fight that desire to scream back. The way to do it properly is to remain calm, breathe deeply, slowly and look the person in the eyes. Let the person finish speaking and repeat what they said in a lower, smooth voice, questioning back if you understood properly their concern. The other person tends to follow and lower their voice also. It may seem strange but it is exactly what happens most of the time because they will feel you understood them.

Let me give you a couple of examples for when your manager is really not happy and screaming at you.

1ˢᵗ EXAMPLE:

Manager (screaming): "You did not finish the work on time yesterday like you said and because of you, the customer will get the product late and I have to hear from my boss"

You (low/calm tone): "So, you are saying that I did not finish the work on time yesterday like I said I would and because of that the customer will get the product late and you have to hear from your boss?"

Manager (not screaming but talking loud still): "Yes that is what I just said." (The tone has gone down a bit)

You (low/calm tone): "The reason I did not finish the work on time yesterday was ………."

2nd EXAMPLE:

Manager (screaming): "You missed a deadline and because of that the part will not be shipped on time and the client is not happy at all."

You (low/calm tone): "So you are not happy that a date was missed and because of that we cannot ship the part in time and the customer is unhappy?"

Manager (not screaming but talking loud still): "Yes that is what I just said." (The tone has gone down a bit)

You (low/calm tone): "The reason the deadline was missed was ……….. and we can still ship to get it on time……"

It seems strange, right? but it works. Of course, you have to explain what happened, but the other person will be much calmer and more receptive to what you have to say. So yes, explain why and have a solution or suggestion to help solve the problem. If you don't have one in mind, that's ok, say you will come back later with an idea or solution.

> The first reason people leave the company is because of their direct manager. People leave the manager not the company.

This is a proven technic used mainly by customer service that really works. I have tried it several times, even at home when in an argument with family members and it will defuse the situation.

TALK WITH YOU ABOUT OTHER PEOPLE BEHIND THEIR BACK

Figure 14 - Photo courtesy of rawpixel.com

This is not acceptable to me and I don't accept this kind of behavior from my team either. We all have talks on the coffee break room about not agreeing with someone in the company but there are 2 situations that you should not tolerate.

SITUATION 1 - If you manage a team and one of your team members comes talking to you about a colleague, just to diminish him or her that is not acceptable. It is ok when they complain about missing deadlines because a colleague is not doing their part on time. What is not ok is to talk about another colleague because of their bad personality or differences or what government party they support or because they don't wash their hands, something on those lines.

SITUATION 2 – Another situation that you should be careful about is when one of your colleagues comes to you to talk badly about your manager. Even if you don't like your manager, don't forget, your job is to support him or her. I don't always agree with my superior decisions and I always express my opinion and concerns. Whatever he decides is the way, he has my full support.

Be careful that there are employees who just want to know what you think about your manager, just to tell your manager what you think about them. They will throw you under the bus and take advantage. If this kind of "coffee break" conversations occurs, just change the subject, leave because you have an important thing to do or just say you don't agree with that line of conversation.

One tip, don't trust people who come to you to talk about others behind their backs. I can assure you, they will do the same thing to you. They are trying to get information about you and what you feel about someone else, so they can use that information against you or have some kind of leverage.

CONGRATULATE YOU

Figure 15 - Photo courtesy of rawpixel.com

Talking about this seems strange, doesn't it? Why am I talking about how to react when someone congratulates you for achievement for example?

Because, if you have passive employees, they hate for you to congratulate them in the presence of others. Even when you congratulate them in private, they tell you a story about how they were able to do that remarkable achievement, and how it was mostly due to their luck or someone else great help and they can go on about how it was very easy, anyone could do it…., etc.

They do it because they don't want to be the center of attention.

If you fit this group, take the credit. You deserve it. Refer to other team members if they were involved and just say thank you. If you don't put yourself on a higher standard, no one will. Stop sabotaging yourself. It is already difficult when you have others trying to make you "bite the dust". Don't help them in their goal by putting yourself down. One of the most important things, if not the most important, is what you say to yourself every day, your inner conversations.

TROUGH YOU UNDER THE BUS

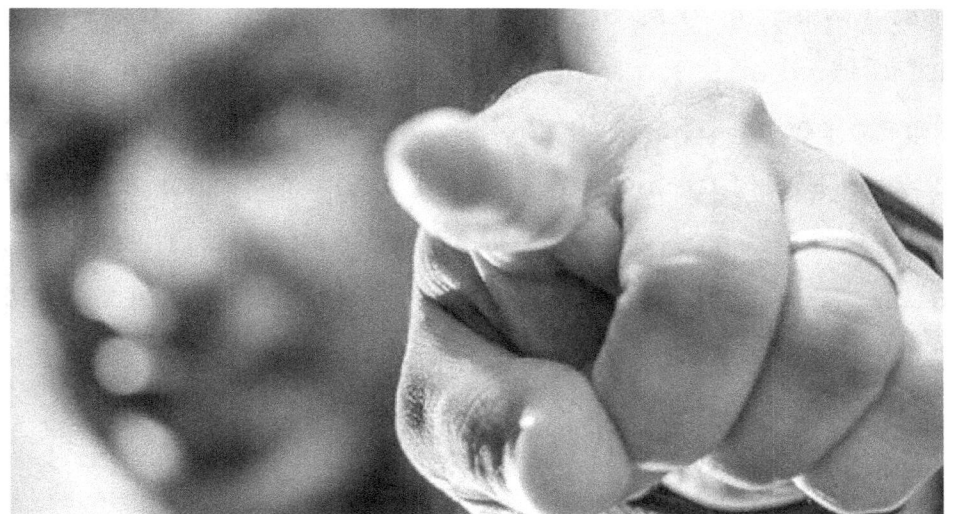

Figure 16 - Photo courtesy of Rodolpho Zanardo

There are employees who will take any chance they have to put you in the spotlight for something you did wrong or to embarrass you. Their objective usually is to gain some kind of advantage, preference or to remove the spotlight from themselves. There are also the ones who do it because it gives them pleasure. They are just bullies.

I had to deal with this kind of person several times in the past and still at the present moment. You will find them everywhere, not only at work.

Let me tell you something that happened to me some time ago. I was called to a meeting with no warning notice and not told what the meeting was about. I got in and there were 5 people at a table looking at me with a very serious look on their faces. They started blaming me for a part of my work I approved which according to them was incorrect. The feeling I had was I was being interrogated by the police. Did this ever happen to you? Were you ever in this situation? How should you react to it?

Use the same technics you would use when someone is screaming at you. Be calm, breath slowly, answer in a smooth way, look in the eyes of the person who is speaking to you and stand straight with your head high.

If you have difficulty looking in someone's eyes, just look right over the person's eyes, focus on his or her eyebrows, forehead or try to see through the person.

Don't trust people that come to you to talk about others behind their back.

You can practice this at home with a family member or a friend.

After listening to what they have to say, explain your point of view, what happened. If you don't have an answer right away it's ok, just say you will look into it and come back in a certain period of time. If it was really a mistake and it was your fault, apologize and mention it will not happen again.

You will be surprised how managers like to have employees that step forward admitting that they failed and have measures to make sure that does not happen again.

People get very tired with all the finger-pointing and with the excuse that it is never his or her fault. This does not mean that every time you make a mistake you are going to announce it to the World. Admit your fault only if you are not able to fix it without being noticed, for example.

Going back to my story, the meeting I was called into. I knew most of those people. When they were alone, not in a group, they never had this kind of behavior with me. Together in a group, they acted like a "gang" because they have no character, no values and only care about themselves.

Don't be surprised if a seemingly supporting person or someone you talk daily on a coffee break, act differently when in a group. You can really see the real character of a person on 3 occasions:

1 – When playing sports (like on a soccer game) with them;
2 – When in a group and "the roof is on fire";
3 – When they are being pushed against a wall and being blamed for something they did.

With experience, you will gain like a sixth sense on how to spot these kinds of people. Do you have a strange feeling at times about someone, something just doesn't fit and you feel it in your stomach and you cannot really put your hand into it? That's the warning sign. You can't rationalize it and say what it is. With experience, you have the ability to know what it is, but even if you don't know, don't disregard your instincts.

DEEP BREATHING EXERCISES

Figure 17 - Photo courtesy of Ingrid Santana

There are several exercises that can do to quickly help you lower your stress and anxiety.

I know of several people who use this website, https://www.therapistaid.com. It is a good resource with different exercises available to you.

Stress and anxiety can really get in your way, more than you think. Let me give you an example. I had a classmate in the University who was very smart, he was an ace in everything he did and he knew the answer to any problem but for some reason instead of having "A"s on the exams, he had "C"s and I never understood why.

After we become good friends and his grades started to improve to "B+" and "A" I asked him why the low grades before. He told me that exams made him so anxious that he would have blanks and not remember the answers to the questions. He hated doing exams. He felt they were very stressful.

Fortunately, he had good parents who noticed the change in his behavior and sent him to a psychologist who helped a lot by giving him some breathing, relaxing exercises and encouragement.

Nowadays he uses the exercises less and less but still has in his wallet a small paper with fast breathing exercises to help him calm down. (Every time he needs it in stressful situations)

Deep breathing is a simple technique that is excellent for managing emotions and to calm you down. Not only is deep breathing effective, it's also discreet and easy to use at any time or place. If you have racing thoughts it will also stop them or slow them down.

One time I saw a video of a Monk explaining what happens inside our head when we meditate and when we do the breathing exercises. He explained we have a "monkey mind". This monkey is always talking, chattering and never shuts up. The only way to calm his chattering is to keep him busy and give him a job to do. Give the monkey mind the job to be aware of your breath.

You can upgrade this technique by doing the breathing exercises and imagining at some time the air entering your nose, filling our lungs and coming out of the mouth. Imagine it is a kind of smoke that goes in and out. Really imagine it going down the tube, filling the lungs and up again. That will keep the "monkey mind" busier. It is normal to have thoughts while doing the breathing exercise, just ignore them and concentrate on your breathing.

So here is one well-known breathing exercise:

Sit comfortably and relax your arms, you can just leave them on top of your legs. Breathe in through your nose, hold the air in your lungs and then exhale slowly through your mouth, with just a small opening on your lips like if you are blowing through a straw.

Do it slowly. Inhale for 4s, pause for another 4s and exhale for 6-8s. Do this for about 3-5 minutes.

Anxiety can be magnified by irrational thoughts. For example, the thought that "something bad will happen" or "I will make a mistake" might lack evidence, but still have an impact on how you feel.

Breathing exercises will lower your anxiety but there is another technique that can help you a lot.

Just write your running thoughts in a paper. In one column write the repetitive thought you have, the one that keeps popping in your head. On a second column write the facts which support that thought. Let's make sure they are not fictitious and you are writing the facts that support that repetitive though. On a third column write a solution and a date for you to solve it. If there is no solution, just write something that comforts you and you know it is true. This technic is used by some psychologists.

Sometimes it is difficult to know why we are feeling in a certain way but remember when you are anxious that means you are afraid of something and when you are sad, that means you feel you have lost something.

Ask yourself what and do the previous exercise.

POCKET READER

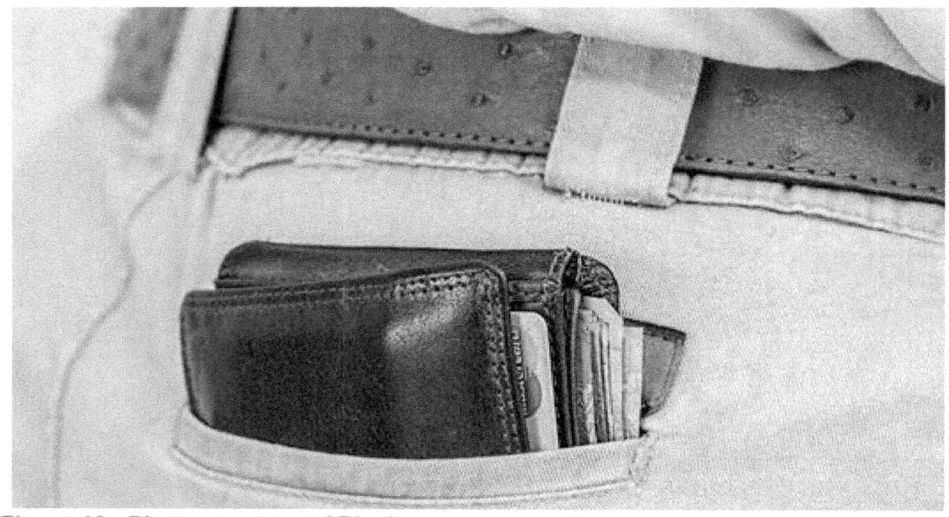

Figure 18 - Photo courtesy of Pixabay

Print the next page in a small format and take it with you, in your wallet for example so it is there whenever you need it.

This will be very handy if you are in a situation you need help controlling your emotions.

I have used it multiple times and it works. Read it slowly and don't rush it. It will calm down your stress, anxiety and racing thoughts.

Deep Breathing

Sit comfortably and relax your arms, you can just leave Them on top of your legs. Breathe in through your nose, hold the air in your lungs and then exhale slowly through your mouth, with just a small opening on your lips like if you are blowing through a straw.

Do it slowly. Inhale for 4s, pause for another 4s and exhale for 6-8s. Do this for about 3-5 minutes.

Racing thoughts

In one column write the repetitive thought you have, the one that keep popping in your head. On a second column write the facts which support that thought. Let's make sure they are not fictitious and you are writing the facts that support that repetitive though. On a third column write a solution and a date for you to solve it.
If there is no solution, just write something that comforts you and you know it is true.

ONLINE TESTS

Figure 19 - Photo courtesy of Kaboompics.com

There are hundreds of tests you can do online to test your EQ but I decided to list here my favorites. It is always good to check where we stand on EQ and then improve it or not depending on the results.

www.verywellmind.com

Psychology-tools.com

Harvard Business - hbr.org/2015/06/quiz-yourself-do-you-lead-with-emotional-intelligence

https://testyourself.psychtests.com/testid/3979

University of California -
https://greatergood.berkeley.edu/quizzes/ei_quiz

University of Center Florida -
http://sciences.ucf.edu/psychology/myemotions-hxus/

EQ CONCLUSION

I hope you enjoyed reading this chapter and you've felt it empowered you. My main purpose is to open your eyes, give you the tools, open your eyes and prepare you for what is out there. If tomorrow you feel a little better, smarter, calmer and in control, then I have fulfilled my mission.

Some say that the work environment is like a jungle. I believe it is more like a chess game and you have to know how to play it well. You need to plan your next move, choose the path you want, the door to open and take chances at times.

Don't be afraid. Select the higher moral ground, be proud of every achievement, be smart and open-minded. Remember in the end it is just a job, do the best you can. Never be caught off guard again, be prepared when action is required.

Chapter 2
HOW TO PREPARE FOR YOUR JOB INTERVIEW

INTRODUCTION

You will be better prepared for an interview when you finish reading this chapter. I will show you how to prepare yourself and succeed in your interview. I will focus more on technical job interviews where I am more experienced but what I mention here applies to many other areas too.

Why do we have job interviews? If we have already all the information about the person, the CV, linked-in profile, recommendation letters, portfolios, and other information. We need job interviews to meet the person face to face, to measure him or her up.

Can't we just then make a phone interview? Even if you have a phone interview it is very important to meet face to face. If you remember from Chapter 1, 55% of the language is body language:

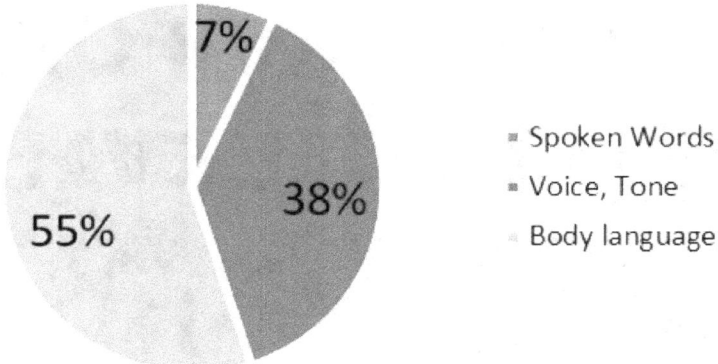

It is also extremely important to meet face to face to ask underlined questions that aren't clear on all the documents supplied by the interviewer and observe his or her reaction.

PREPARE FOR YOUR INTERVIEW

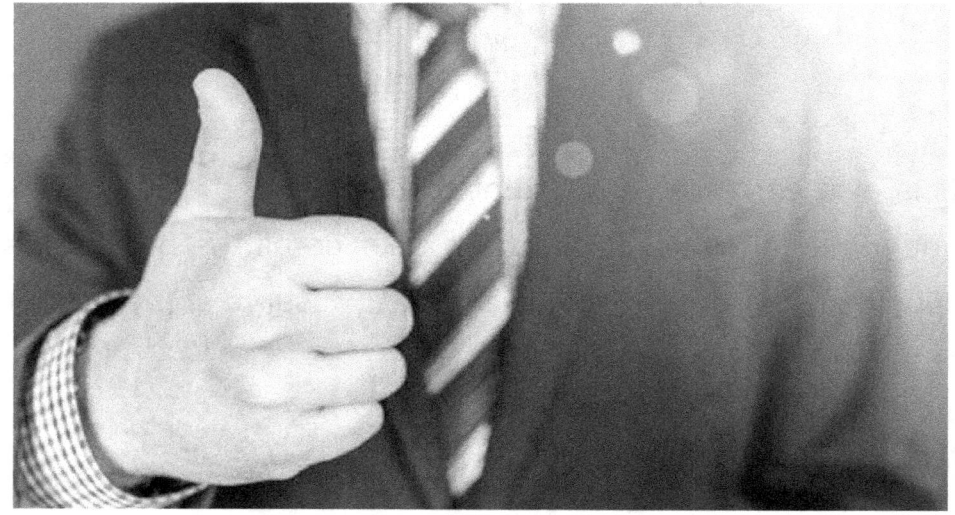

Figure 20 - Photo courtesy of Lukas

Let me show you how you should prepare yourself for an interview. There are several things you need to work on to be prepared for an interview, the CV, the way you dress and your posture. There are other important topics I will refer to here, that will help you get the job you want or reject the job you don't want.

Don't underestimate the importance of all these things in your interview and remember the interview goes both ways. It is a way for the interviewers to meet you and for you to meet them. They need you on that spot in order for them to be successful.

Be prepared to say you are not interested. Some companies with bad intentions will try to undermine you and make you feel they are great and you are lucky if they hire you with a low paycheck. We'll see that more in detail moving forward.

APPLY TO THE CORRECT JOB OPPORTUNITY

Figure 21 - Photo courtesy of rawpixel.com

What do I mean about the correct job opportunity? I have seen it before where people lose lots of time replying to a specific job advertisement that they have no chance to get. So what should you do to make sure it is the opportunity that fits you and you are looking for?

First, read in detail what is required on the job advertisement, the qualifications and most importantly what is required for you to do and the level of experience expected. Your CV does not need to match 100% what is required in the job advertisement. Typically they request the "perfect" candidate who usually does not exist.

Be sure you have the main qualities required. You can learn the rest of them later.

Secondly, be sure you like the location and then go online and check how much this job pay is usually. You can go to www.glassdoor.com or www.payscale.com, for example, and get an idea.

If the job advertisement has a number or email contact, be free to ask for more information like salary range and benefits. If there is no contact information that's ok, the benefits and salary are usually discussed in the first interview with HR.

PREPARE YOUR CV AND PRESENTATION LETTER

Figure 22 - Photo courtesy of Lukas

There are countless different ways you can write a CV and format it. Let me give you some clues and directions on how to write a proper CV that will gain the attention of the recruiter.

Have a maximum of 2-3 pages on your CV. Recruiters don't have time to look into very long CVs. Keep it simple and only the relevant and latest experiences. It does not make much sense if you are applying for a manager position, for example, to still have on your CV that you're worked 15 years ago in the University library. When recruiters get hundreds of CVs a simple, well-structured CV is taken more into consideration. Have on the top of your CV your contact and photo (optional), and a second part talking shortly about your experience, followed by your Areas of Expertise, Courses, degrees and at the end all the professional experience and significant achievements.

I see different formats being used in different countries and they tend to follow a certain standard. For example, in some Countries, the photo on the CV is essential on others optional or even perceived as discriminatory.

One thing I found in common is many people using the same CV format for all the job offers they apply to. If one job advertisement asks for experience in program management for example and you have that down on your CV, bring it up to the top of your CV, add as more detail as possible and emphasis it. This will strike the recruiter's eyes immediately.

Remember, HR looks at your CV first. They will do the first triage and then give their chosen one to the manager hiring. The manager will let HR know which candidates to pursuit. Having that in mind, be sure to have all which is mentioned on the job offer that match with your experience on the CV and in more detail. Don't forget to include your achievements.

To help you create your CV I found two websites I really like, www.novoresume.com and www.zety.com. They will give you a good jump start.

The presentation letter is also very important. Contrary to your CV which shows your experience and qualifications in chronological order, on your presentation letter you should start by presenting yourself, writing shortly about who you are, your experience and then highlight and go into more detail on the experience you have that match the job advertisement. There's no need to emphasize your other experiences. Be sure to hand sign in the end and to put a date on the top of the page.

THE FIRST INTERVIEW

Figure 23 - Photo courtesy of rawpixel.com

Usually you have the first interview with HR before you have are with your future manager. Nowadays the first interview is normally done by phone or video-conference.

The phone is the most used way of communication for the interview. You can use this way of communication to your advantage because you can get lots of information, and take some paperwork with you. This way you can have a quick look at the information you need without the interviewer's knowledge.

For the phone interview go to a quiet room, take your CV, the information about the company that you are applying to and the job advertisement. Underline any important information on those documents that you think are relevant.
Keep calm during the interview, answer the questions with a firm tone and take your time when answering back. Remember, 38% of the communication is transmitted through voice and tone.

Some companies are now doing the first interview by video conference. There are several services you can use for video conference but the one I am familiar with since my company uses it is www.HireVue.com. HR is responsible for the video conference and then giving it to the manager. Then the manager watches the recorded video interview and assesses candidate competencies all in a single step.

By using the Video interview way of communication, HR is trying to have the whole pie on types of communication. If you remember from chapter 1, 7% of the communication is spoken words, 38% is voice and tone and 55% is body language.

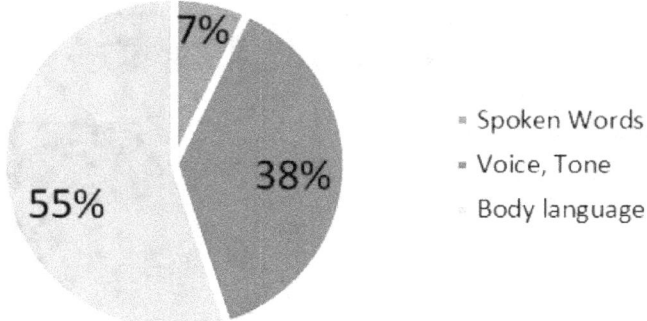

Be sure you are prepared for the video conference interview. Perceive the video conference as a face to face interview. Choose a room where there are no distractions like TV noise or people talking. Sit preferably at a desk in a quiet place with a wall or bookshelves behind you.

Make a video test call to a friend or family member to make sure nothing goes wrong during the interview. I have seen it happen before where the sound is not working or you cannot see the other person on the screen. Prepare the best you can for all to go as smooth as possible.

DRESS CODE AND POSTURE

Figure 24 - Photo courtesy of mentatdgt

First impressions are important and you have a window of 30 minutes, maybe one hour, to make the best impression you can at your face to face interview. Normally by the way people dress and their posture, I can take some hints on how the person is going to be at its job. So don't disregard the importance of it,

55% of the language is body language.

it can mean the difference between getting the job or not.

Imagine you are trying to get a role in a play and you are auditing. You only have a few minutes on stage to give all you got to catch the recruiter's attention and curiosity. So anything positive that can help get their attention, you should use it.

DRESS CODE

Figure 25 - Photo courtesy of Fancycrave.com

The way you dress and present yourself is extremely important. You should dress accordingly to a job you are trying to get. If you are trying to get the job for a fashion magazine, for example, you have to look fashionable with nice clothes, haircut, and accessories. If you are applying for an engineering opening, dress sharp or smart casual, don't overdress and look like you are going to a wedding. If on the other hand, for example, you are trying to get a position for the shop floor just dress causal with a clean look.

So what kind of signals do I get from the way candidate dresses for an interview? Remember, I am in the Engineering business so let's imagine I am hiring a design engineer. First impressions can change later on during the interview. They can fade away or be more evident.

If a candidate overdresses wearing a suit, tie, and shiny shoes, it is usually because of one of three scenarios:

1 - The candidate likes to dress sharp. It is his or her style. There is nothing wrong with that.

2 – The candidate wants to impress and overdresses;

3 – The candidate is using his or her looks as a smokescreen. Probably he or she doesn't have the qualifications needed to do the job. Normally I ask a lot of technical questions to try to get the "smoke curtain" to fade.

On the other hand, if you have a candidate that dresses too sloppy, lacking on personal hygiene, it is usually because of 2 scenarios:

1 – The candidate is going to be sloppy on the job too;

2 – The candidate is going through a rough phase on his or her personal life and that is going to interfere with their performance. I have empathy for people passing through a rough phase but my job is to hire the best professional that can do the best job.

POSTURE

Figure 26 - Photo courtesy of Bruce Mars

Your posture sends a message to your interviewer, so it is important that you use the correct one. Remember, 55% of our language is body language. Having that in mind, start by walking straight, keep calm and look people in the eyes when talking to them. Some people find it hard to look people in the eyes. If you find it difficult too, look to the eyebrows or through the person, imagining what it is behind him or her.

Practice this with someone you know or in front of the mirror while at home and believe me people will never know the difference.

Now let me show you what your posture should be during the interview.

Don't **sit** sloppily. You show a lack of energy and engagement. Don't sit on the edge of the chair because it shows you want to get out as soon as possible, are nervous or tense. Don't lean back on the chair because it is too casual. Don't site sideways, it shows the interviewers you are not comfortable with them.

Sit straight on the chair, leaning forward just a little towards your interviewer. It shows interest, that you are actually listening and involved. One last tip, keep your head straight.

Put your **hands** together on your lap or on the table in front of you. Avoid touching your face or having them above your neck. They signal the interviewer you are lying or anxious.

Don't wave your arms and hands around too much or fold them across your chest in a defensive manner.

Try to imitate the **body language** of your interviewer. Most of the time, at the beginning of the interview, their body posture is very formal but tends to become more informal during the interview. You should do the same and by doing that you will establish harmony.

Don't cross your legs or do many movements with them. It shows you are too casual or nervous. Keep your legs straight, parallel with both feet on the ground.

Make eye contact but don't stare. Blink your eyes from time to time. Look at the eyes for 10 seconds and then look at the interviewer's forehead for a microsecond and come back to the eyes. The listener is the one that has to keep eye contact for longer. The speaker is the one who will do the eye shift. If you have more than one interviewer, direct your eye contact to the person who asked you the questions but then look at the others for a second and go back to the speaker so you involve everyone.

Keep your voice calm, make pauses to breathe, don't talk too fast and avoid monotony. Try to keep the voice tone and pattern as the one of your interviewers.

Lastly, control your emotions. Avoid laughing too loud, making extreme expressions and moving your arms and hands a lot. Keep calm, smile and nod your head a little when time is appropriate.

INTERVIEWER BODY LANGUAGE

Figure 27 - Photo courtesy of Bruce Mars

No one is perfect or behaves the same all the time. Sometimes we make mistakes or say the wrong thing. We don't have a crystal ball to know how the interviewer will react to that but there are certain signs that you can spot on the interviewer that will help you notice when something is wrong and move right back on track.

I will show you 5 situations you can easily practice at home and memorize so you will be prepared when they happen. Do some role-play at home with a family member or a friend.

So let's learn than 5 situations which I like you to be stick to your brain.

SITUATION 1 – INTERVIEWER RAISES THE EYEBROWS AND OPENS THE EYES WIDER

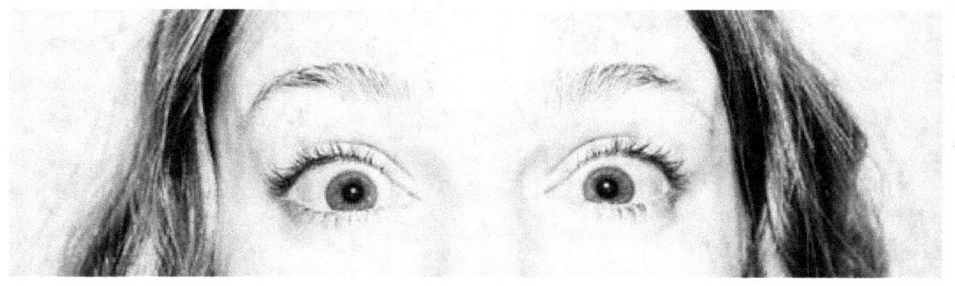

Figure 28 - Photo courtesy of Tookapic

Usually, when this happens, they don't believe what you've just said or are surprised by your statement. Never lie in an interview. You must be ready to support your arguments with facts. So, if you notice your interviewer is having this behavior, explain to him or her, the facts.

SITUATION 2 – INTERVIEWER IS RESTLESS, TAPS THE FINGERS ON THE TABLE

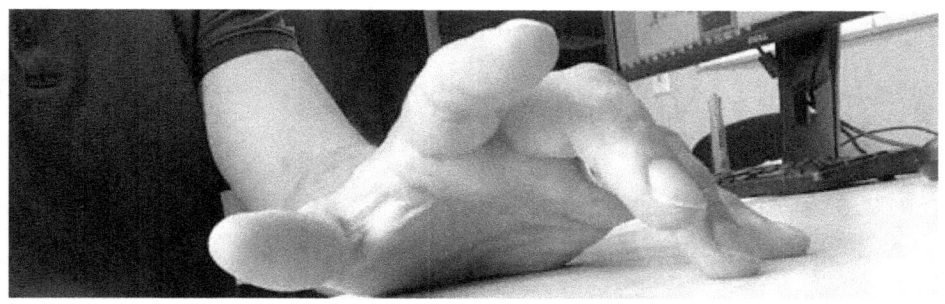

The interviewer is frustrated and that usually happens when your answer is not quite what he or she expected or is out of bounds. Maybe you did not understand the question, so stop and ask back politely if what he or she asked was this or that.

SITUATION 3 – INTERVIEWER HAS CLAMPED LIPS AND IS FROWNING

Figure 29 - Photo courtesy of Andrew Dick

The interviewer is confused or does not agree completely with what you are saying. Finish what you are saying but in the end, don't forget to ask if they need clarification or more information.

Never ask the interviewer if he or she understood you. Always ask if what you said was clear. Put the ball on your side don't blame the interviewer for any misunderstanding.

SITUATION 4 – INTERVIEWER CROSSES ARMS AND LEANS AWAY FROM YOU

Figure 30 - Photo courtesy of SplitShire

Most of the times that means you are too close to the interviewer and he or she feels uncomfortable. Try to step back or somehow create some distance between yourselves. He or she may also react like this because you said something rude or asked a personal question. Avoid this kind of situation by being polite all the time.

SITUATION 5 – LOSES EYE CONTACT AND ACTS RESTLESS

Figure 31 - Photo courtesy of rawpixel.com

Probably you are giving a very long answer and not going straight to the point. Just finish what you are saying and gain their attention by asking a good question.

QUESTION THE INTERVIEWER

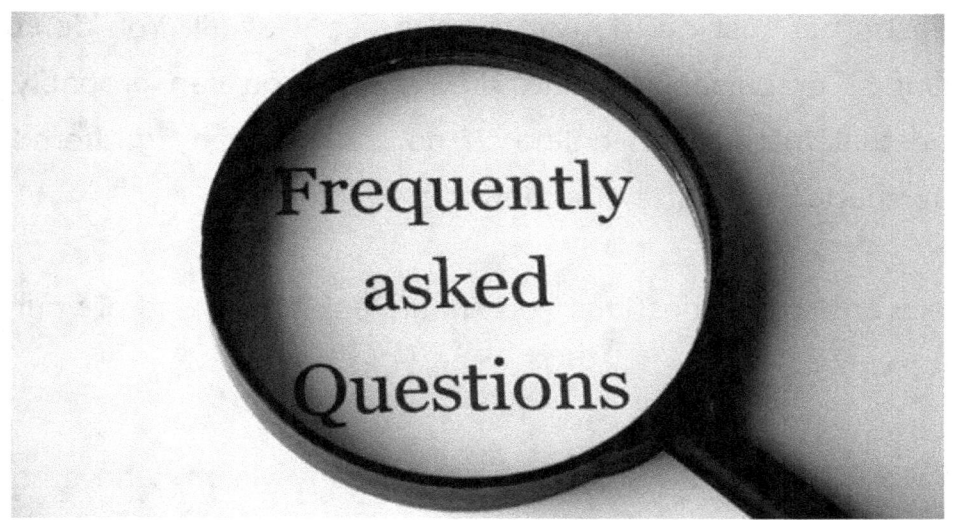

Figure 32 - Photo courtesy of Pixabay.com

At the end of the interview usually the interviewers will ask you if you have any questions for them. You should have some questions in advance because it shows you went prepared, that you're interested in getting that position and reminds the interviewers, even if in a subtle way, that this is a two-way street and you are also there to interview them. You are valuable and you need to be sure that this job will satisfy your needs and expectations.

If the interviewer seems to show he or she does not know the answer to your question, go easy when rephrasing the question or just decide not to rephrase it at all. You don't want to embarrass the interviewer and you can probably find that information online. If not, you already gathered information from the interviewer's reaction.

Here are some questions you should ask at the end of your interview:

QUESTION 1 – Ask what is the company vision, where he or she thinks it will be in 5-10 years. This will give you a glance of this being or not a safe company to work at and if you have a chance to advance on your career.

QUESTION 2 – If you would like to try working in several places worldwide, ask the interviewer what other branches they have Worldwide.

QUESTION 3 – Tell the interviewer that you are very ambitious, want to rise on the company tree and if there is a place for you to grow on the company. This will show them that you are a hardworking professional, with very specific goals and if they do not meet your expectations you will probably end up leaving the company. This question can also protect you from being hired into a company where the employees like to slack on the job or where people step on each other to move up on their career. Knowing you are a hard-working professional and that you could easily impress their bosses and thus take their jobs, they will not hire you. You don't want to work in a company where you have this kind of moral and environment. Look for a healthier company where working as a team can be fun and fulfilling.

QUESTION 4 – Ask about the size of the team you will be working with, the number of hours a week and if the company has a flexible schedule.

QUESTION 5 – If you need a VISA and the company will take care of that for you, ask if they will also help you to get the permanent resident status.

QUESTION 6 – You may need to travel. Ask how frequently and for how long is expected for you to travel especially if you have a family. Nowadays the more you move up on the company tree the more it is expected for you to do some traveling. The question is how much traveling is ok for you?

QUESTION 7 – Ask about your benefits, what they are and what the relocation package is if you move from another state or Country.

QUESTION 8 – Ask the interviewer when you can expect their contact and when do they need you to start if you are selected.

QUESTION 9 – End by asking if they have any more questions for you.

SALARY AND BENEFITS

Figure 33 - Photo courtesy of Alexander Mills

Some job advertisements in the newspaper or online already tell you the range of salary they are offering but nowadays it is a rare thing and usually, you don't see that in the advertisements. Sometimes you get an offer from the recruiter but most of the time they will ask you how much you presently earn and

> Never ask the interviewer if they understood you, always ask if you were clear enough.

how much you expect to get. They are trying to have your talent at their disposal for as little as possible. It is nothing personal it is just how companies operate.

I was asked several times what my current salary was at my previous job. I don't agree with the question, I think it's invasive, unethical and it is even illegal in some US states. Recruiters want this information so they can give you an offer slightly above what you are getting. The objective is to make you happy just with enough.

I was asked the question when I was working in the UK. I asked back why they needed that information and why it was that relevant for the new position. The HR woman on the other side stutters for a second and then had lots of things to say and excuses. None made sense to me.

When this happens be sure to:

- know your state's or country's salary history laws and remind the company who is interviewing you that the question is illegal;

- change the subject, talk about the salary requirement and not the history of it. Give the salary range you are expecting based on your experience and education.

- Share your salary history if the range offered by the company is lower than what you are making now. In this case, it will be an advantage to disclose the salary history.

So how do you know what the fare salary is for your new possible position? There are several websites that will help you with that, the ones I usually use are Glassdoor.com, Salary.com, and PayScale.com.

If you are going to several interviews for the same type of positions you can and should reveal what other companies are willing to pay you to try to raise the salary they are offering you.

If you are moving to a parallel position in another US state or country, there are websites that show you the difference in the cost of life on those states/countries and how much you should get to keep the same lifestyle. Here are the most useful websites with some examples:

C2ER – US COMPARISON - $8 Cost

https://store.coli.org/compare.asp

This one goes really to the detail of showing you the price difference for everyday items.

Item		Price 1	Price 2	Price 3
Ground Beef		$3.51	$3.82	$3.8
Sausage		$3.97	$3.84	$3.9
Frying Chicken		$1.26	$2.46	$1.4
Chunk Light Tuna		$0.82	$1.09	$1.0
Whole Milk		$1.45	$1.92	$2.0
Eggs		$1.10	$1.73	$1.5
Margarine		$0.94	$1.35	$1.1
Parmesan Cheese		$3.64	$4.70	$4.0
Potatoes		$2.73	$3.57	$3.0
Bananas		$0.57	$0.72	$0.5
Lettuce		$1.28	$1.66	$1.3
Bread		$3.35	$3.46	$3.2

BANKRATE – US COMPARISON - FREE

https://www.bankrate.com/calculators/savings/moving-cost-of-living-calculator.aspx

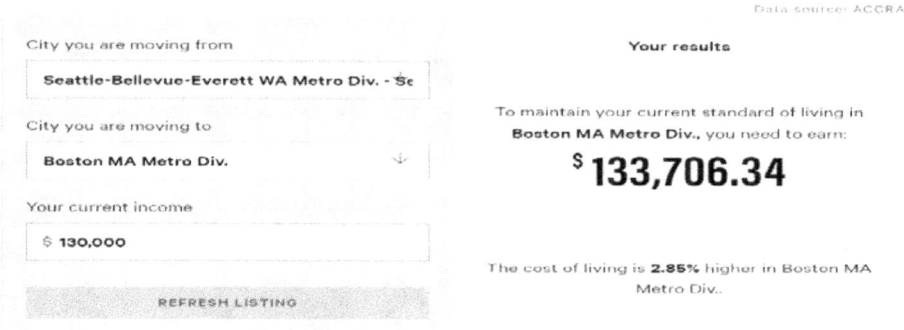

NUMBEO– US COMPARISON - FREE

https://www.numbeo.com/cost-of-living/comparison.jsp

BEST PLACES– US COMPARISON - FREE

https://www.bestplaces.net/cost-of-living/

2019 Cost of Living Calculator:
Seattle, Washington vs Boston, Massachusetts
Change cities

A salary of **$130,000 in Seattle, Washington could decrease to $115,725 in Boston, Massachusetts** (assumptions include Homeowner, no Child Care, and Taxes are not considered. Click here to customize.)

Comparison Highlights
- Overall, Boston, Massachusetts is 11.0% cheaper than Seattle, Washington
- Median Home Cost is the biggest factor in the cost of living difference.
- Median Home Cost is 22% cheaper in Boston.

NUMBEO–INTERNATIONAL COMPARISON - FREE

https://www.numbeo.com/cost-of-living/compare_countries.jsp

Cost of Living Comparison Between London and Boston, MA

You would need around 5,001.76£ (6,333.40$) in Boston, MA to maintain the same standard of life that you can have with 4,700.00£ in London (assuming you rent in both cities). This calculation uses our Cost of Living Plus Rent Index to compare cost of living. This assumes net earnings (after income tax). You can change the amount in this calculation.

Indices Difference
Consumer Prices in Boston, MA are 7.70% **higher** than in London
Consumer Prices Including Rent in Boston, MA are 6.42% **higher** than in London
Rent Prices in Boston, MA are 4.80% **higher** than in London
Restaurant Prices in Boston, MA are 2.47% **lower** than in London
Groceries Prices in Boston, MA are 56.86% **higher** than in London
Local Purchasing Power in Boston, MA is 48.14% **higher** than in London

Currency: GBP ▼   Sticky Currency   Switch to metric measurement units

They have different results because they look at different parameters. Used them all and get the best salary possible.

Chapter 3
HOW TO DO A PROPER JOB INTERVIEW

INTRODUCTION

On Chapter 2 I talked about how to be prepared for an interview, on this chapter I will show you how to be prepared to give one instead.

I will show you how to prepare an interview with the proper steps to optimize your time and other parties involved. Like I mentioned before, I will focus on technical job interviews where I am most experienced, but you can apply these technics to other departments also.

Let me remind you that it is extremely important to meet in person so you will be able to read his or her body language. Ask underlined questions not found on the support documentation and observe the candidate's reaction.

PREPARE FOR YOUR INTERVIEW

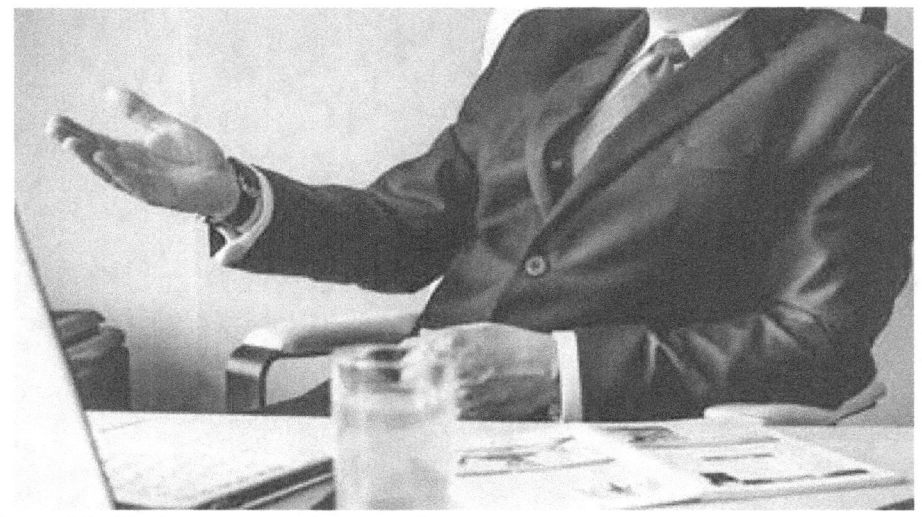

Figure 34 - Photo courtesy of energepic.com

I met professionals who believed they didn't need to be ready to give an interview or were too busy to do so. They just needed the CVs and since they had a lot of experience, they just went with the flow. Well, in my experience if you don't prepare yourself for the interview you are about to give, you miss things and eventually lose the perfect candidate for the job or even hire the wrong one.

It's a shame not to hire the perfect candidate because you didn't take the time to prepare yourself. You probably don't even notice it when it happens. What you probably did was to give the perfect candidate to the competition.

On the other hand, if you hiring the wrong candidate will damage your company, decrease office morale and eventually lead to losing customers. Layoff employees cost a lot of money to the company and can be easily avoided.

I had to lay off an employee because he was like a sea of negativity and it was damaging my team performance and morale. Unfortunately, this was one of those cases where I inherited this employee from a previous manager.

JOB ADVERTISEMENT

Figure 35 - Photo courtesy of Pixabay.com

You need to work with HR in order to find the perfect candidate. Don't try to do it by yourself because HR knows how to word it properly but don't let HR do it all by themselves also. They don't have your expertise and they don't have a clue of what you are looking for.

According to me there are types of candidates easily identified:

- **THE PERFECT CANDIDATE** has all the experience and skills you are looking for, only needs minimal training and can start working full engaged from day one. Tell HR who the perfect candidate is for you, the one who fits like a glove.

- **THE GOOD CANDIDATE** requires some training but has the majority of experience and skills you are looking for to fill the position. Usually, 1-3 month training will be required until he or she gets to speed.

- **THE BEGINNER** requires a lot of training and does not have much experience. He is willing to learn and his or her motivation makes him or her a good candidate if you have the time to train him or her properly. Their training usually takes 3-6 months depending on the complexity of the work required.

- **THE GRADUATE**, straight from the University. This candidate is a long term option. It usually takes one year of training until he or she is ready to have minimal supervision on medium size projects.

The correct candidate for your vacancy depends on when do you need him or her to be ready and up to speed, accounting the time you are going to need to train the new employee. You need to think in terms of salary vs training. Lower experience means a lower salary but more training will be required. On the other hand, higher experience means a higher salary and less training will be required. It is all about delivering something with quality, on time at a low cost, right?

The following pie chart shows the types of candidates hired in my company. This is based in a pool of 175 Engineers hired to a medium-complex vacancy. I compared the results with other companies and the results are very similar.

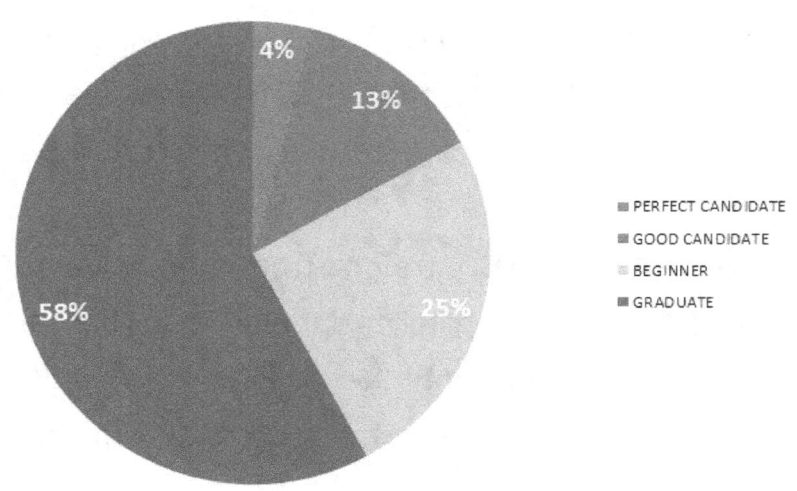

When I am looking for a new candidate I contact HR and tell them who the perfect candidate is for me and the 2nd best option. Usually, the perfect candidate is hard to find and most of the time the position is filled by the 2nd best option.

Let me share a story that happened to me where things didn't work as planned.

One time I was asked by a colleague to help interview a candidate for his department. After interviewing the candidate I knew he would not fit the available position. This was a high articulated candidate, straight out from the university. I was looking for a candidate with a minimum of 3 years' experience for my department and I decided to hire this candidate. Why?

He didn't have the knowledge or experience, but I liked his honesty, intelligence, engagement, and determination. He was a mechanical engineer and I was looking for an electrical one, so he did not have even the correct college degree.

I took a chance. I had 3 months to test him and tell HR if I wanted to keep him and I did. He was up to speed not in a 1 year but in 6 months, he was super smart, a very fast learner, curious, motivated and grateful for the chance I gave him.

I always prefer a motivated smart candidate who you can mold and train rather than an experienced one with no motivation, full of bad habits, just looking for a job.

CV PYRAMID

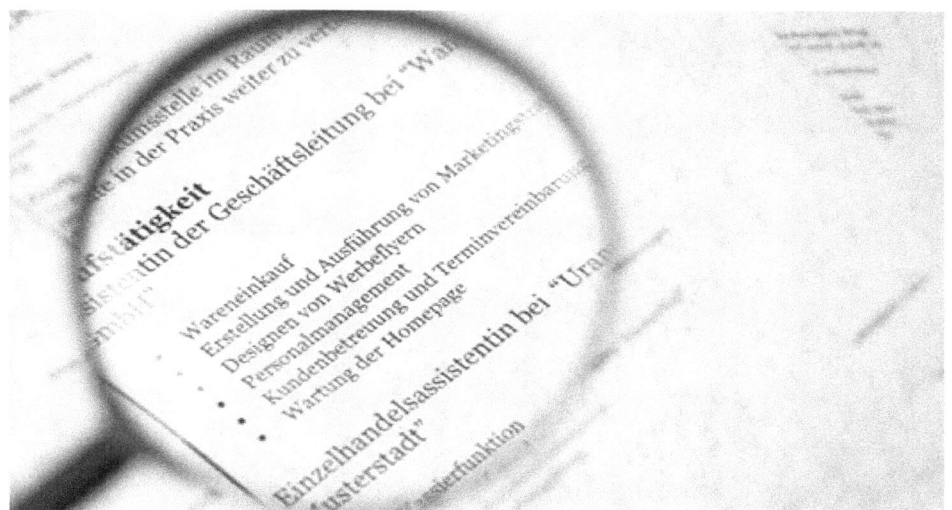

Figure 36 - Photo courtesy of Pixabay

Look at the CVs with scrutiny. Print a copy and take notes on it. Look at the CVs and decide whom of those candidates you will meet in person, face to face. Choose the best 3 for one vacancy. There is a lot of time and money involved to prepare a face to face interview, so be sure you are thorough.

How do you quickly filter through all the CVs?. Let's follow the CV PYRAMID method, which I designed and from which I obtained successful results, to quickly find the best candidates for an interview.

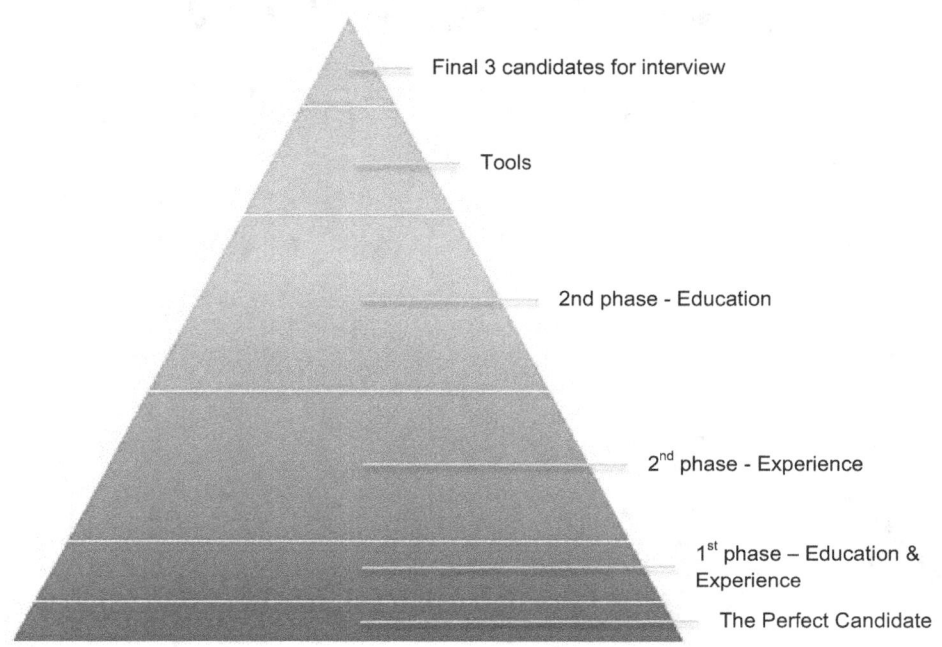

The Pyramid shows all the phases you need to go through, from down to up, until you get to the last 3 candidates.

As an example, let's says you have 20 CVs to go through for one vacancy.

THE "WHITE WHALE", THE PERFECT CANDIDATE

These candidates are rare, but let's say you find one. Don't just call HR right away, singing with joy that you found the one. Remember, having the perfect CV does not necessary being fit for the job. You need to have a face to face interview.

Now let's move on and imagine we don't have any perfect candidate and we still have 20 candidates left to go.

1ˢᵀ PHASE EDUCATION AND EXPERIENCE
(20 CVS TO GO)

So we have these 20 CVs on hand. The second thing to do is to check if the candidates have the correct, desired degree and job experience.

Did they finish their degree? Just take a quick look at the CVs without looking at how many years of experience and what degree they obtained, just a very broad look.

These are all the relevant things you should look at first. If HR did their job correctly, they should have only handled your CVs that have the correct qualifications and experience but mistakes are made. This exercise will probably make you discard +/- 10% of the CVs.

This was the easiest part, it is really a black and white exercise. So let's say from the 20 CVs we are now left with 18 CVs.

2ND PHASE EXPERIENCE
(18 CVS LEFT)

Now that we have "separated the wheat from the chaff" let's take the remaining 18 CVs and grind down until we're left with only 10 CVs.

Go through the remaining 18 CVs and set aside the 10 CVs that have a better experience. Better experience can mean several things like, for example, how long they performed a certain role in a company. I like a candidate who has had a role in a company for at least 3 years and not a candidate who jumps to a new company or position every year.

In my opinion, experience should mean the types of projects the candidate was involved in, doing what, for which companies and on which fields. This varies, depending on what you are looking for.

2ND PHASE EDUCATION
(10 CVS LEFT)

Now that you have 10 CVs left to go select the top 5 with the most relevant education, better degrees, courses and certifications relevant to your vacancy.

TOOLS
(5 CVS LEFT)

With 5 CVs left to choose the 3 that will need less training on specific tools you use, like specific software for instance.

Now that you have your 3 top candidates lets prepare the face to face interview.

PREPARE THE INTERVIEW

Figure 37 - Photo courtesy of rawpixel.com

Now that you only have 3 CVs on hands and have communicated that to the HR, they will contact all 3 for a face to face, phone call or a video call interview. Whatever way your company operates, on this next step you need to be prepared for the interview.

Don't just go to the interview unprepared with the CV in front of you. You will miss things and if it is a face to face interview you will show the candidate that you didn't care enough to be prepared since you will be reading the CV back and forth looking for things to ask.

Reading the CV back and forth also takes your eyes from the candidate and you're not able to evaluate properly his or her body language.

Grab one CV at a time and highlight in green the experiences, degrees and courses you would like to question him or her about and that are relevant to the vacancy.

Highlight in blue to signal all training in software and hardware you think is relevant for the vacancy.

For last, highlight in red all the things you doubt, don't understand on the CV or just seem strange to you.

I knew a candidate who mentioned on the CV he graduated a 4 years course in 2 years. This is the kind of thing you should be asking about.

Take notes on any information you can grab about the companies they worked for. Check if any of them ring a bell because maybe you know someone from those companies you can ask for references. We live in a Small

World. I had candidates who knew people working on my company so that makes things easier because you can ask your colleagues what they think about the candidate.

Another thing you should be looking for on the CVs are gaps in time, periods of time when the candidate wasn't employed. It is ok for people to take time off work but ask why in a certain period they were not working. It could have been for health issues, just time off or for a failed attempt of trying to be an entrepreneur but it did not work.

> If you hire the wrong candidate, it will damage your business, change office moral and you can lose customers.

I once had a candidate who I asked why she had a gap of 6 months on her CV and she answered me she didn't feel like working, she needed a break. Well, that's fine, but the way she said it, in an "I don't care" way, raised a flag to me. That made me think that this candidate probably wasn't very responsible, could quit the job anytime, not show up for work or just do the bare minimum.

On the next pages, you'll find some examples of questions you can ask during an interview. I wrote these questions down thinking I was hiring an engineer for a supervisor role and I wanted to focus on his or her leadership capabilities. You can take some hints from these questions, modify them and use them in diverse areas.

Print the questions and take them with you. Write down the answers and what you observe during the interview in regards to the body language and voice tone. Don't think too much when you write it down, you can review your notes later.

Remember the answers you want to hear from the candidate are not just yes or no answers. Encourage the candidate to talk as much as possible about a variety of situations. Listen and observe his or her responses closely.

Review chapter 1 about emotional intelligence. Check also chapter 2 especially the topic about "Posture" and "Read the interviewer body language". These will help you read and understand the body language of the candidate during the interview. Remember if the candidate's body language says one thing and verbal another, body language is the one truthful.

Engineer Leadership Interview Questions

Candidate:_____ Date:_____

1. **What was the biggest team you lead and on what kind of projects were you involved?**

Answer:
_____
_____
_____
_____
_____
_____
_____

Body Language/Voice Tone:
_____
_____
_____
_____

2. **Did you lead a cross-functional team and/or multicultural team? If so please give a couple of examples.**

Answer:
_____
_____

Body Language/Voice Tone:

3. **Please tell us about the time you had fewer resources on your team and you were required to finish the project in time. How did you handle the situation?**

Answer:

Body Language/Voice Tone:

_____
_____

4. Tell us about the time you had more resources on your team than required for the projects at hand. How did you handle the situation? What did you do with the extra resources?

Answer:
_____
_____
_____
_____
_____
_____

Body Language/Voice Tone:
_____
_____
_____
_____

5. Tell us about the areas of your job where you believe you excel. Where do you feel you need improvement to increase your effectiveness on the job?

Answer:

Excel_____
_____
_____
_____
_____

Needs_____
_____
_____
_____
_____

Body Language/Voice Tone:
_____
_____
_____
_____

6. Describe one normal day supervising your team and especially how you keep track of the work being done, deadlines and assign new work. Give an example.

Answer:
_____
_____
_____
_____
_____

Body Language/Voice Tone:

_____
_____
_____
_____

7. **Please tell us in detail about the things you've enjoyed doing in your current and past positions. How about the things you have not liked in those jobs?**

Answer:

Like_____
_____
_____
_____
_____
_____

Dislike_____
_____
_____
_____
_____
_____

Body Language/Voice Tone:
_____
_____

8. Give examples of how you reward a team member for a good job done and of how you deal with a difficult one that does not do the minimum necessary for the position.

Answer:

Body Language/Voice Tone:

9. Explain to us your method to evaluate your team performance and assign goals.

Answer:

Body Language/Voice Tone:

10. Describe a situation where you took full responsibility for actions and outcomes of errors caused by you and/or your team that impacted a specific project. Tell us what happened and how did you prevent that from happening again?

Answer:

Body Language/Voice Tone:

11. Tell us about a time when you were proud of your ability to be objective and avoid being

emotionally involved even when you were in a situation that you were feeling emotional.

Answer:
_____
_____
_____
_____
_____
_____

Body Language/Voice Tone:
_____
_____
_____
_____

12. Give us an example of a goal you reached that seemed difficult to reach and how you achieved it. What tools, techniques, strengths, and knowledge you use to get there?

Answer:
_____
_____
_____
_____
_____
_____

Body Language/Voice Tone:

_____
_____
_____
_____

13. Describe a time your work was rightly and wrongly criticized. Why were you criticized and how did you react?

Answer:
_____
_____
_____
_____
_____
_____

Body Language/Voice Tone:
_____
_____
_____
_____

14. Describe an occasion where you had to listen to another person's point of view in order to solve a problem or to deal with an issue. What was the problem/issue?

Answer:

Body Language/Voice Tone:

15. Describe a situation where an engineer came to you with a problem that involved other stakeholders in different countries, the issues were urgent and you could not contact those stakeholders due to time difference. How did you handle the situation?

Answer:

Body Language/Voice Tone:

16. Please give an example of a time when you demonstrated a sense of urgency about getting results.

Answer:
_____
_____
_____
_____
_____
_____

Body Language/Voice Tone:
_____
_____
_____
_____

THE INTERVIEW

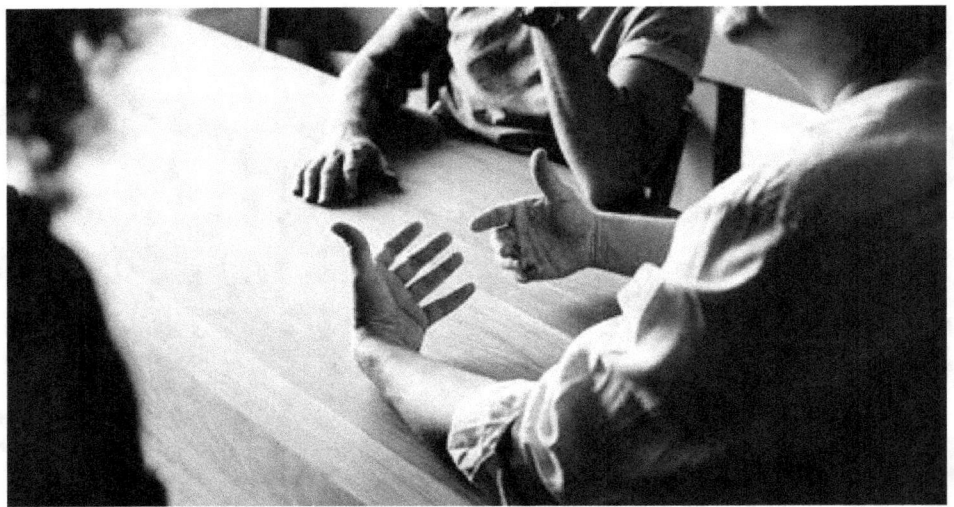

Figure 38 - Photo courtesy of rawpixel.com

On this subject I will focus on face to face interviews only. You can use what I am going to mention here in phone and video interviews. Just leave out what does not apply like, for example, if I speak about analyzing the body language you cannot do that on a phone interview.

Be sure the room is prepared appropriately and on time. Make sure it has the proper room temperature, bottles of water available, paper and pens and projector ready and tested if you are going to use it to make a presentation about the company.

I read some articles about companies that opt to use a round table instead of the common rectangular one. I can see why some companies choose to use a round table. It makes the interview meeting less formal and more relaxed. In my opinion, using the round table makes it very difficult to read the person you are interviewing, to read properly his or her body language. I like the round table concept for team meetings perhaps but for an interview, I prefer the rectangular where the candidate is on one side and the interviewer is on the other.

Invite other parties for the interview if you think their input is valuable. If you have a counterpart on the company take him or her also to support you. You take notes for example while the counterpart asks questions.

Finally, let's talk about how the interview day should roll out. Receive the person on that day. Go meet him or her at the front desk of the office. Offer coffee,

> Always prefer a motivated smart candidate that you can mold and train that an experienced one with no motivation, just looking for a job.

water or refreshment and have a small talk about if he or she had difficulty finding the office, how the trip went, anything, just a relaxed conversation to calm down the "guest" and make him or her feel comfortable. Yes, they are your guests and should be treated as such. Take mental notes of the body language and write it down when you get to the meeting room as soon as you have a chance. Present the other interviewers to your guest and ask him or her to sit down.

Start by making a presentation of yourself and everyone in the room. After that, ask the guest to introduce himself or herself. Ask why he or she answered to that position and what they know about your company.

Next, do a company presentation. You can just do an oral presentation or use the projector for a short slide show presentation. Try to keep it on a maximum of 15min long. Talk about the role and what you expect from the candidate who takes the position.

Now you can start asking the questions you've prepared before and taking notes of the answers, body language and voice tone. When you and all the other interviewers are finished, ask the guest if he or she has any questions.

In the end inform what is going to happen next, on what time frame they will be contacted and escort the guest to the front door. Ask if a taxi is needed, shake hands and go back to the meeting room to discuss how the meeting went with the other interviewers and what are their thoughts on the candidate.

WRAPPING UP

It was really a pleasure writing this book. Thank you for choosing it. I really hope you enjoyed it and that you will take to your workplace what you just read here.

For me, it is very fulfilling to be able to help others get better results, be stronger and sharper. I hope when you finish this book you feel like your vision is wider and that you will be able to find things that are not so easy to see at first.

If you apply the information present in this book you will be able to move up faster on your career. Others will notice that you look "taller", different, more mature and will consider you a great asset to the company.

Control your emotions. You cannot control other's emotions but you can influence them in your favor.

Be free to contact me at uyourp@gmail.com or go to my website www.uyourp.com if you want more information or have any questions.

Thank you very much. Don't forget to keep an eye at volume 2 in which I will write about all aspects of team management and make you a respectful leader.

FREE DOWNLOAD

Contrary to popular belief, your resume and presentation letter will not get you that desired job opportunity. Use this free document to help you prepare for the interview and keep them organized at the same time.

Sign up for the author´s New Releases mailing list and get a free copy of the "Get a Job organizer"

Click here to get started https://www.uyourp.com/job-interview-organizer/

www.ingramcontent.com/pod-product-compliance
Lightning Source LLC
Chambersburg PA
CBHW060839220526
45466CB00003B/1173